Very
Practical
MEDITATION

Very Practical MEDITATION

Serene West

Donning
Virginia Beach/Norfolk

Cover art by Fischback & Edenton

The Donning Company/Publishers
5659 Virginia Beach Blvd.
Norfolk, Virginia 23502.

Library of Congress Cataloging in Publication Data

West, Serene, 1929-
    Very practical meditation.

    (A Unilaw library book)
    1. Meditation.   I.   Title.
BL627.W44   158'.1   79-20249
ISBN 0-89865-006-2

Printed in the United States of America

TABLE OF CONTENTS

INTRODUCTION

Meditation is simply a continuous thought of God or good held in the mind. Meditation can be quite practical and beneficial to every area of living, and can be just as meaningful in the kitchen as the cathedral.

Why should we suffer unnecessarily? By emptying our mind of worry thoughts, and holding a thought of good, our lives are elevated and we are able to overcome mountains of frustrations, seeming limitations and fears.

Often the missing key in meditation is faith. Without faith, there can be no success. Some years ago, I wrote an article, "Alarm Clock Faith," which was published by *Weekly Unity*. the theme was centered around the fact that we put complete faith in the workings of a $5.95 alarm clock, relying solely upon it to arouse us for our most important appointments, as well as the job which provides us with the necessities of living itself. It's fine to have faith in an alarm clock. I give thanks for mine! And we can learn a very elementary lesson in faith from our alarm clocks! So let's lift that "alarm clock" faith up and put it to work in our daily lives and meditations. Let's put faith into whatever we picture for ourselves.

I feel that I should also post a warning against giving up too soon. If after a few sessions of meditations, your dreams haven't come true, don't quit! It is my belief that we receive just the amount of healing, prosperity and happiness that we can accept at the time. As we expand our spiritual awareness, we will be able to accept increasingly more.

My reason for writing this book is to share with you, the reader, the wonderful truth about the power of creative thought. I know the power.

In the fall of the year 1976, I became stricken, almost overnight, with rheumatoid arthritis. For a year I suffered day and night, even though I would not give up my work or activities. I was totally shocked and confused as to why *I* had been so cursed! Then one day, it came to me that I knew better and I must do better. I continued under a doctor's care, but I began a program of daily picturing myself agile and free from pain. I saw myself dancing, doing leaps across a grassy lawn, running, typing and all the things which I so wanted to do. All the while, I was being given stronger and stronger medicine. Finally when I was put on Prednisone, the pain left. But I knew that this medicine was damaging my body temple. I was led to change doctors. He kept me on the Prednisone, and I was wondering *why* I had been led to change doctors. But never doubt your strong feelings if they persist. Eventually, I grew to understand.

The new doctor was a rheumatologist. My former doctor had not been. Under the rheumatologist, my diet was changed, my shoes were made more comfortable with a bar to relieve the pressure on the ball of the foot, and I noticed that the pain marks were beginning to leave my face. This all left me in a state in which I could better concentrate during my meditations. I meditated constantly and one year later, I was off all medicine completely and doing all the things that I wanted and needed to do once again.

Creative thought is a magic wand! Creative imagery can change illness into health; fear into freedom; timidity into self-confidence; and failure into success.

Many of you are familiar with this true story, but it bears repeating, for it remains to be my very favorite illustration of true believing.

A young couple was talking one evening after dinner about the mice that they had been seeing around their home. They decided to do something to get rid of them as soon as they could get to the nearest pharmacy for a supply of poison. Now the young son, who had a child-like love for all living things, cringed at the very thought! He had been attending a Sunday School and had learned an offering blessing. It was the only prayer that he had ever been taught. He remembered from Sunday School that if he prayed, believing, his prayer would be answered. So he prayed several times a day that the mice would leave his home and go to their right place. But this was the prayer that he used:

> *"Bless and multiply*
> *All that I give*
> *And all that I receive."*

His prayers were answered. The prayer of his heart—not the prayer which he mouthed. The mice disappeared.

What we truly, truly believe will surely come to pass—if not in one week—then one year—or ten years! Never, never give up! But we have to be honest with ourselves, for what is in the heart is what counts.

I would feel so honored by you, dear reader, if you would use this book as a textbook, (certainly not *the* textbook, but one of several, perhaps) underlining words and phrases that are important to you. I would like for you to feel that we are working together for perfect communication with our Creator, ourselves, and each other.

Know that as I meditate, I will ask for each of you deeper insight and courage. As you read this book, I can almost promise changes for the good for you, *if* you read with your heart. This is a heart book—it was written from my heart.

Serene S. West

Foreword

Meditation is the way back to the most precious part of our being. That part which has never been touched on this road of life we all travel. In meditation we find peace and balance and realize that there is much more to us than meets the physical eye. Much comes forth from that quiet place to strengthen and enhance our everyday living experience, and all of Life takes on a more meaningful dimension for us.

—Anne Francis

PART I

Learning to Meditate

Learning to Meditate

Meditation is as natural as breathing. But we have gotten away from the natural in a "follow the leader" and "get with it" world. It is natural to make contact with the source of your being. There is yearning to return to our oneness with All-Good. But sometimes we walk around and around missing "the path" by mere inches. We are in the dark without a match, it seems — and the feeling is one of restlessness and frustration.

It was just such a state that caused Matthew to ring my doorbell early one autumn morning and plead with me to help him find some peace of mind. His problems were many. He did need help.

In the kitchen over a quick breakfast I explained to my young friend that I was not a professional counselor, even though I had done much teaching, lecturing and writing.

"Perhaps you should go to a professional counselor," I suggested.

He stubbornly refused and just sat there looking miserable.

"All right," I finally agreed, "I will help you as a friend."

He relaxed somewhat and we talked about his goals and deep desires. I knew that I could not solve his problems

—only he could do that, but I could help him to learn the ways of meditation. So it was agreed upon that he would come every day after I had returned from my day of teaching and, as his friend, I would try to guide him in the path that I had walked so many, many years.

Meditation proved to be the answer for Matthew. His entire life was changed.

"And I thought that when you suggested meditation I was in for a complicated and maybe boring experience! Man, this is so easy and *natural!*" Matthew exclaimed, near the end of our meetings. "Hey, maybe you should write a book on how easy meditation is!"

Well, I did just that, and Part I is devoted to the steps that young Matthew went through. Hopefully these steps will help you realize also that meditation *is* easy. It is natural. It can be life changing!

Let's follow Matthew through his early days of meditation.

1st Day:

"Where do you think you would be most comfortable?" I asked Matthew as we stood in the middle of my living room. "I'd like for you to choose a place that you would like to have as your special spot *every* time."

Matthew looked around slowly and went over to a straight ladder-back chair.

"Nobody sits in that chair," I laughingly told him. "That chair is a decorative piece — a whim of mine. Please don't plan to torture yourself. You don't have to be uncomfortable in order to meditate."

Matthew looked relieved, laughed good-naturedly and took an armchair. He slumped down — looking somewhat like a strawman.

"Well, not *too* comfortable, either!" I chided him.

Matthew found that by placing his feet on the floor and his hands on the armrests, he was relaxed and comfortable, yet alert.

"Now, close your eyes," I instructed, "and let go. Let every worry, every anxiety leave quietly with no arguing from you. You cannot handle them anyway, so let them go —one by one. Now relax and breathe in slowly. You are breathing in life — abundant life. Give thanks for it. Know that this life is everywhere in the universe. It is divine — therefore, you are a divine being. Breathe and relax. Breathe and let go. In — out — in — out — slowly.

Now relax the shoulders. They are tight from carrying so many burdens and fears. Imagine that they are being relieved of their burden. You do not need to carry these heavy burdens any longer. You are a divine being."

By now Matthew was totally and completely relaxed.

"Open the palms of your hands, Matthew. Be ready to receive your own good. Open hands are the symbol of receptivity — the willingness to receive," I reminded him.

Matthew wanted to go into deep meditation that day, but I stopped the lesson right here.

"Don't rush," I told him again and again. "You are making progress. Now I want you to practice. Walk outside, then come back to your chair and go through the steps of relaxation."

He did practice — while I started dinner for my family. I heard him open and close the door several times, so I knew he sincerely wanted help and was willing to carry his load of the responsibility.

2nd Day:

The next afternoon Matthew was eager to get to the next step. He went immediately to "his chair," sat down — back straight, feet on floor, arms on armrests, with palms opened upward — eyes closed and began the soft slow breathing.

"Let your breath say, 'Life! Life!' as you inhale and exhale," I suggested.

When I could see that Matthew was relaxed, I whispered softly to him:

"Matthew, you are created in the image of God. Your greatest desire is to know this — to really know it! You want to feel that oneness with God. You want to *feel* the warmth of God's perfect love. You want to *feel* the excitement of life flowing through your body. You want to *know* the power that strengthens and overcomes. You want to express God's wisdom — understanding and perfect judgment. You want God's perfect order established in your life. Say to yourself 'I and the Father are one' — God moves in and through me —we are one."

I left Matthew alone for a few minutes as he grasped the ideas I had presented. When I returned I asked him to slowly open his eyes and join me in the kitchen.

"How do you feel?" I asked him as he walked into my kitchen.

"My problems aren't solved yet," he answered, "but I do feel more relaxed and peaceful."

"Well, you know you didn't get all of those problems in a day. It just might take a few days to shed them!" I said.

Yes, ma'am, I know. I guess I'm impatient. See you tomorrow."

As I watched Matthew leave, I knew he wanted to do more. He expected more from me. I knew I had to try to get him to see the beauty of simplicity and sincerity.

3rd Day:

By this third day Matthew was familiar with our simple routine. He settled himself quickly in his "meditating chair" and went through the steps of complete relaxation.

"Today try meditating on *love*," I suggested. "Think about any phase of love — love of children for their parents — love of teachers for their students — love of sister for brother — parental love — devotion of pets — yet bear in mind, Matthew, that it is all *love* and comes from God."

Matthew nodded and began.

Up to this point we had kept the meditations rather short. As I extended it a mere five minutes, I could see Matthew starting to squirm a bit. As we walked into the kitchen I asked him to tell me how he felt near the end of his meditation time.

"I kept thinking about going to the bathroom!" he told me in a joking manner. "*And* my nose itched — my back ached — I was just jittery! I guess underneath it all I'm not very spiritual, am I?" he stated openly.

"Oh, but you are!" I assured him. "If you weren't spiritually developed, you wouldn't even be here! It is your body demanding equal time that is causing you all the discomforts. Your body is not used to sitting still for so long. It is trying to get your attention. All you need to do is talk to it lovingly and firmly — it will cooperate.''

4th Day:

"When can I start telling God my problems?'' Matthew asked hopefully shortly after he arrived. "I have some 'beauts' and I really would like to get them rolling!''

"There is *no need* to tell God your problem. Just know that it is solved and thank God for it!'' I answered him.

Matthew looked at me skeptically.

"All right — I know that's vague. But would you be willing to try this, Matthew? Every time this so-called problem comes to mind, think of God in some phase. You will have to do it *deliberately.* Turn your thoughts from the problem to thoughts of God.''

"Okay — I'll try it,'' Matthew said, "but what about my regular meditation?''

"There are many, many, many forms and methods of meditation, Matthew — just as there are many, many, many kinds of food. Take and use the one needed at the time. All meditation is contact and communion with God, right?'' Matthew nodded. "Well then,'' I continued, "as you turn from problem-thinking to thinking of the glory of God, isn't that meditation too?''

"Sure,'' Matthew agreed, "but I could be standing up —even on the job — or on a date — ''

"You can meditate *anyway* — *anytime,* but you still need your meditation chair for regular daily meditation. By the way, Matthew, do you have a meditation chair at home?''

"Why, no — '' he answered and looked truly shocked! "I've just been using *your* chair, you know — ''

And we both laughed like good friends should. But Matthew got the point.

5th Day:

Matthew was so excited as he came bounding up the walk. He was early and I was spending a few minutes in my yard.

"I tried it and it worked!'' he told me excitedly. "You know — the turning away from the problem thoughts and thinking about God. It really worked!"

"Why sure," I answered. "It has worked for me too."

"I hope it works every time! It's like magic! I've got it made if it works every time!" Matthew told me in happy tones.

"Was it *that* good?" I asked.

"Sure! You see my aunt had asked me to take my cousin back to school this weekend. Well, I know it's not the Christian way to feel — but the truth is I *detest* being with that girl. She's always putting me down, if you know what I mean. And she's a chain smoker. I have a new car and the thoughts of her smoking it up just turns me off! It's brag — brag —brag and then this putting me down — I just can't stand it! She really does bug me! Anyway, there just wasn't much I could do about it — there didn't seem to be any way I could get out of it without causing a family 'flap.' It was depressing me and ruining my day. Then I started thinking about God as Life everywhere around me whenever the thoughts of that trip with 'cousin' came to mind. It only took one day before my aunt called me and said she'd decided to take Diedre back herself and go visit some relatives. How about that?"

"That's great — for now!" I answered. "And maybe the next time you're asked to drive Diedre you will be so sure of your own self that she can't 'put you down' and also you will be able to say 'No smoking in my new car, Cousin!' "

"Maybe," Matthew replied thoughtfully.

We walked around the yard and pulled weeds from the flower beds that day and talked. Now Matthew knew of two ways of meditation — there are many! Yet he didn't quite know *what* meditation was. Matthew had in mind that meditation was a kind of magic or mystical experience. He was to learn that meditation is simply channeling the mind Godward. If the mind strays it can be gently and lovingly brought back in line. Since God is Love, Life, Perfection and Perfect Peace, we are free to choose any quality of God to think upon.

6th Day:

Matthew knew that meditation *did* work by now. He was beginning to feel more optimistic and confident of the future. He was less dependent upon me as a spiritual guide.

There was more going on inside than outside. So it was on this day that I asked Matthew to jot down some of the experiences on the meditative path. He did so wholeheartedly and I share them now with you.

7th Day:
    I felt relaxed today —
    Kept thinking about the new shoes in the window —
    Pulled thoughts back in —
    Very relaxed and happy —
    Realized the world is *good* when I'm happy —
    God is good —
    God *is* good and I am some good, I know.
    We are one.
    I felt it today — we are one!
    I almost slipped into sleep.
    Good meditation —

8th Day:
    I was tense —
    Needed meditation badly today —
    Still going around and around even after what seemed to be a long time —
    "Why can't I relax?" I kept asking myself.
    Finally began to unwind —
    !?*!! — my foot itched!
    Talked to body —
    Asked the Lord of my being to calm me down —
    Other foot itched — oh, well —
    Breathed slowly and repeatedly —
    Thought of God's Perfect Peace —
    Perfect Peace —
    I was swept up into a high state of awareness at last —
    It was worth waiting for —
    I am grateful.

9th Day:
    Almost felt that I didn't need to meditate today!
    Everything fantastic!

Beautiful array of colors during meditation —
Felt loved — secure — warm —
Meditated in joy!

10th Day:

I was happy today — others not so —
Realized the need for patience —
Dwelled upon God's love — not like human love —
God's love eternal — pure — constant —
Asked to be one with Perfect Love —
Good meditation.

11th Day:

Had problem — determined not to let it interfere —
Had hard time relaxing —
Problem came to mind —
Turned it over to God —
Relaxed —
Light flashed — jarred me —
(What was that?)
Relaxed deeper —
Good meditation.

This was the first day that Matthew had shown concern about anything that he had experienced in meditation.

"It was like a giant flash bulb going off before my closed eyes — yet it seemed to be from within — not without," he stated.

"Yes, that has happened to me many times," I assured him. Yet I could not really explain this to Matthew. Who really knows? Who can call himself an authority? What causes the flashing light that many have told me about? My own feeling is that it is just that — a flash of light — a flash of insight — of knowing. It has seemed that way to me and I am cheered each time the light flashes for me — or for others.

12th Day:

Matthew handed me his sheet of notes, then sat down as if ready to discuss something.

"What is it, Matthew?" I finally asked him.

"I want a mantra," he answered simply. "Several of my friends are in T. M. and they say a mantra is absolutely necessary."

"Well, a mantra isn't *absolutely* necessary for meditation, in my opinion, but it does help. A mantra is an aid — nothing more. We might say it is a flashlight opening up the way in the dark tunnel — or perhaps more like a friendly guiding hand. But Matthew wanted one, so we discussed its merits.

A mantra is one word or a group of words that we hold on to when we feel jittery or begin wandering mentally during meditation — then it suddenly came to me that I myself had a mantra. My mantra, is a group of words — or really a thought. I can go into meditation very quickly and very easily as I hold this thought of oneness with the Creator. Sometimes I repeat these words silently: "I and the Father are one — I am part of God. He is all of me. We are *one.*"

These words convey the idea that I am one with my Lord. Being one, I feel the attributes of His perfect nature, I feel perfect love, abundant life, good health, wisdom and wealth.

I shared my "thought" mantra with Matthew and explained to him how we should each choose our own. He did, and just as I suggested, he did not share it with me, although he did tell me it was just one word.

Armed with his mantra and his newly found technique of meditation, Matthew moved with his family to another city many, many miles away. I wondered if he would become discouraged, or tire of meditation during this change. He did not — and even decided to enroll in the college in his new home town! He was successful in every way — a college degree — a lovely and loving wife — a fulfilling career — and finally a family. He is still meditating and attributes all that he is to the fact that he meditates daily. Best of all, he is teaching a young men's class in his church the importance of daily meditation.

After working with Matthew, I helped several others in the beginning stages of meditation. But let me be quick to say that one can only be guided in meditation. It can not be forced. It must be *deeply* desired.

11

Elizabeth thought that meditation was an easy way out. She heard of others getting fantastic results from meditation and she wanted these same results, so she sat quietly for thirty minutes every day — for years — but with no results!

Elizabeth came to me to find out what was wrong with her when she was doing *exactly* what everybody else was doing!

It took awhile to find out what the problem was. It was the fact that Elizabeth's meditations were sterile and consequently they bore no fruit. Elizabeth felt nothing — *absolutely nothing* — in meditation. She sat in a near-sleep state and rested her body. That was all!

There must be an awareness — a certain stirring — during true meditation. We must feel that we are merged with good and love and life. We must be "plugged in," so to speak.

However, we do not need to strain for this. It comes quite naturally *if* there is desire and receptivity. We spend much time each day communicating with our fellow beings — sometimes we are enlightened and sometimes confused.

When we turn within in sincere meditation, we can be sure of finding all that we seek and more. Thanks to the power of meditation, if you are unhappy, you don't have to stay that way. If you are sick — you can experience wholeness and health again. If you are fighting poverty — that too can be changed. You can become as wealthy as you like.

The Bible states it over and over again: "Ask, and it shall be given..." (Matthew 7:7) "...According to your faith be it unto you." (Matthew 9:29) "...When you pray believe that ye receive them, and ye shall have them." (Mark 11:24)

Perhaps the majority of people have not looked into these promises because they did not feel worthy. Perhaps mankind has set the "Good Book" high on the shelf and really not thought of these truths as being personal in any way. Yet throughout time there have always been some who did prove that we can be whatever we desire and have whatever we desire!

William James, father of American psychology, stated that the power to move the world is in your subconscious mind. And what you are doing and being right now is due to what is stored in your subconscious mind.

The subconscious mind can be changed through sincere and constant meditation. These are the two key words: *sincere* and *constant.*

In the remainder of this book I will share two techniques of meditation. The first technique is quite simple. It involves stillness and concentration. The second technique centers around visualization of that which we want to manifest. It too is simple. Both, as you will learn, are *very practical!*

Can I, or any one else tell you how to meditate? Can another tell you how to eat? The answer to both questions may be a "limited" yes — only up to a point. Our parents dutifully teach us correct table manners, how to cut up our foods, which are the wise choices, etc. But, there it stops. We must learn to chew and swallow for ourselves. We must allow our wonderful bodies to do the work in digesting the food we eat. Likewise, we may take classes in meditation, read books and articles on meditation, or take advice from others, on how to best meditate — but here it stops also. Each one of us must feel the presence of the Divine within our own body temple. No one can go all the way with us, for that is holy ground.

Meditation and prayer changes things. Most of all it changes us! Indeed, Universal Law *never* changes. Divine love never changes — divine order never changes — The Principle of Faith never changes. What changes is the error within us as we turn our thoughts to perfection. That is truly the secret of meditation — the turning from hate to love — from confusion to order — from negative to positive — from the seeming problem to good.

Let us become aware of the fact that we attract to ourselves those relationships that irritate and annoy us. When, through spiritual development, we can rid ourselves of our difficulty, then no more will we be bothered by that type of relationship. In like manner, that which we try to own and possess will be taken from us. So we must learn to hold lightly and freely that which we want to enjoy. The cure for jealousy is self-love; so there is little need to blame the third person in the triangle, is there? Learn to love self — not the ego but rather the divine, child-of-God self. When we learn to appreciate our own self, then others will be drawn to us in a natural way. And, of course, when we begin to realize that all are one in brotherhood, our jealousy of others will diminish. Meditation will help us to realize these truths.

There is no need to be frightened of meditation; no need to spend great sums of money for teachers; no need to make it a complicated affair; for meditation comes to all of us naturally and easily. It is our birthright to communicate with the Creator of our being. Get still and turn to God — it's that simple.

Does it work? Yes, it works. Though there are many people who only half believe, or who may believe it may work for other people, but not for them. It always works. Believe.

The first technique in this book deals mainly with attitudes and emotions. As you use the meditations in Part II, please realize that they are only guides. I hope that you will be inspired to write your own as the need arises. Allow your inner self to absorb — to chant and sing into the feeling or idea given. This is an inside job, and no one else need ever know. Relax — let go — be blessed!

PART II

Very Practical Meditations

Boredom and Frustration

I have bottled up within myself thoughts of restlessness — feelings of limitation. Now these negative thoughts and feelings are causing me inharmony and unhappiness. I take the lid off and let them escape — one by one.

As these foreign thoughts and feelings leave me, I feel free and at ease. Now I let the natural feelings of love, joy, and life rise up from the depths of my being. I am content once more. No matter where I am at this moment, I see beauty around me. If I am not where I want to be, I know that I am only passing through — that there is a blessing here for me — and that it is my privilege to be a blessing in this time and place.

I can never be bored or frustrated as I allow God-Mind to flow through my personal mind. God-Mind inspires me to rise above all outer circumstances.

I am rising. I am filled with the joy of life eternal. I am free.

Disappointment In A Friend

Yes, my heart does seem to ache — to feel much like an empty tin box. I trusted, and it seems as if I have been betrayed.

Yet I know that no one else holds me by puppet strings. I hold the strings myself. No one else — no matter how dear to me in the past or even now — can manipulate me unless I have unwisely given this one control.

I am too important to God to give someone else control over my being. My Father-God needs me. I am important to His world.

Therefore, this moment I bless the friend who seems not to need my friendship. But I am needed — my highest, best self is needed.

Thank You, Father-God, for Your constant, endearing love for me. Even when we fail each other in our earthly friendships, Your love encompasses us all. And Your love in me ever draws to me new friends that add to my already happy and well-rounded life. I am grateful!

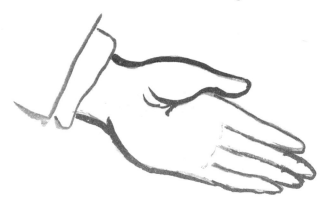

Feeling Pity For Another

I hush the weeping of my soul. I still myself and know.

I know that even though this condition that I have witnessed seems so tragic, there is yet in the very midst of it the presence of God.

God is present to heal — to enfold — to be a comfort — to give hope.

I cease questioning — I cease reasoning — I do not blame — I do not even wonder. I know that here is another child of God — a child in seeming trouble — a child experiencing growing pains perhaps. It is not for me to judge. Certainly it is not for me to pity.

Any feeling of pity now gives way to compassion and faith and I relax — knowing that God in His great wisdom lets each of us work out our own salvation. Yet God never deserts us, for He dwells within and about us all. Who ever could I pity? God indwells all!

Overcoming Fear Of Poverty

I let go such thoughts as, "Will there be enough for tomorrow?" and, "Will I have to do without?" I wholly accept the truth that God is my supply, which never diminishes.

I look skyward. Are the clouds limited in number? No, for even as I gaze upon them, some are dividing and thus multiplying. Do the trees of the forest wear scanty foliage? No, they are all dressed in kingly array! And by night the stars glisten as precious stones upon black velvet space.

So I see that nothing in nature is poverty-stricken. Nothing is limited. One tree does not have less leaves because another has more. One rosebush does not bloom poorly because another blooms in profusion.

I acknowledge the good that I desire. I know that it exists for me — else I would not have so deeply desired it.

I feel plenty pressing against me — I see plenty coming to me in my inner vision — I can now act as if plenty is mine, for I know that in truth it is!

Thank You, Father!

Overcoming Restlessness

This state of restlessness is trying to tell me something. I stop pacing — mentally as well as physically. I still my drumming emotions as well as my drumming fingers. I quiet my racing mind.

I become aware of the vast amount of energy that is welling up within me — energy of life! I am restless because I need to express this life force within me in a constructive satisfying manner.

I now direct this life energy to good; I lift it up to God. This energy is the fuel that feeds some special talent or ability. I am quiet; I listen for an idea; I give thanks for all ideas and thoughts from God-Mind, and for the energy which puts them into action.

Perhaps now is the time to write a letter, or a poem. Now could be the time to make that important decision — to begin a long-put-off task — to volunteer for a service — to dream — to visualize perfection — to begin the climb upward.

My energy is finding constructive use. I rest in God.

Overcoming Anxiety For A Loved One

To my question, "Where is my loved one now long overdue?", I hear the answer: "Enfolded in the love and presence of God."

To any fear that may grip and twist my heart, I hear these words: "Fear not — be still and know."

I now release all to God, for we are all His. I do not personally own a child, a son or daughter. My mate does not belong to me personally. My friends, my family, all people everywhere are all spiritual beings — free beings. Each one is working out his life as he best understands it at this moment. With "hands-off," I release my loved ones to God's care. It is my privilege, however, to surround my dear ones in my mind's eye with the golden light of understanding, love, and wisdom.

I see my loved ones in this healing glow now. I myself am healed of anxiety as I hold out for them a bit of "the light of the world."

Getting Rid Of The "Grumps"

How could a child of God possibly be grumpy and out-of-sorts? I ask myself this question now, yet at the same time things still do seem out-of-sorts.

Just as debris finally comes to the surface of an otherwise peaceful and pure lake, I realize that buried negation has now risen to the surface of my being. It is marring the peace of my soul.

I now banish this negation — no matter whether it emerged from the hidden recesses of my consciousness, or whether it was tossed upon the waters of my thoughts by another. I refuse to allow it to stay. I remove it forever. It has no power over me.

Every cell of my body is alight with the light of pure Spirit. I feel light, joyous, and free. I am the beautiful, calm, and peace-filled expression of God that I was created to be.

To "Loose And Let Go" Another

I have seen imperfection in another and it is staining my soul. I have let another cause me to entertain thoughts which are less than good. I acknowledge the need to let go of the imperfection I have held in my mind and therein free this one and myself as well.

I now see this one in the light of divine spirit. I see no imperfection whatsoever, but rather a whole and pure spiritual being.

Divine love wells up in my heart and flows freely to this one. The rod of negation which has connected us snaps and frees us both. We are each free with the freedom of Spirit.

I praise goodness, love and righteousness. I praise perfection and peace forever.

For Dieting

I realize that my real hunger and thirst is for truth. Perhaps there is some area in my life that is barren and I am trying to fill it in the outer. This craving I have to overeat is not the answer, however. I can be truly satisfied only from within.

I now turn to Spirit to fill the void in my life. I am filled and satisfied as I commune with my Creator-God.

I see my body as the magnificent holy temple that it is in truth. I would maintain it with the greatest of reverence and care.

I listen intently to the voice of Spirit within, which tells me exactly what is needed in my body temple.

I am calm and relaxed as I unfold in perfect understanding. I am filled with joy! I am filled with love! I am filled with peace! I am completely satisfied and content.

When Parenthood Seems Trying

I feel cluttered with care — unappreciated — and overworked. I need to put my house in order.

I go quietly within myself and firmly close the door. I am alone with my Creator — my spiritual Father-Mother.

I know that my Father-Mother God appreciates and loves me. I am all that my Creator is. I am wisdom. I am strength. I am love. I am faith. I am joy. I am power. I am all good in expression.

Whatever quality I need in order to be a wise and understanding earthly parent, I possess. This task that lies before me is a short one, actually. I am equal to the task, for I am not alone. I am a channel through which truth and love flow to my children.

Truly I am a privileged one upon the earth. Thank You, God!

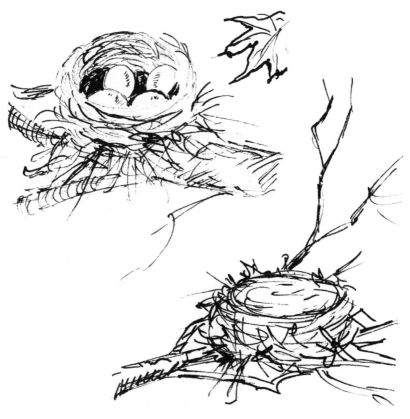

When Another Appears
To Be Able To Withhold My Good

When another appears to be holding my good, I may be tempted to flatter — to connive — to bargain. This is unnecessary! For no one can possibly keep the good that belongs to me! This is divine law and I believe in divine law completely.

I now release any power that I have falsely given to another. God alone is the one source of power. God-Power may work through another, but the source is God always.

I do not need to flatter, cajole, or beg Spirit for my good. All good is already mine — all that I will ever need!

Therefore, my work is spiritual. I must ready myself to receive. I must be filled with faith and know that I am my Father-God's child. My spiritual birth certificate is my faith.

I bless all others that God chooses to work through — but I ever keep in mind the only true source of all my good. I claim my good now!

Seeking The Right Work

God has designated a very special place for all His children — so there is a place for me that meets my needs perfectly — a place where all of my talents, interests, and abilities can be expressed fully and purposefully.

I give thanks for the work that is mine alone to do.

I prepare myself for my right place by doing my best now. Even though I may not like what I am now involved in doing — this is my opportunity to prove my integrity, my honesty, my courage and good will.

All that I do helps me to grow. Every bit of work that I perform adds to my wealth of experience.

I give thanks for work. It is divine. I open myself to new opportunities, knowing that my own will come to me.

Attracting Right Companionship

I attract to myself that which is like myself — so if I would have companions with high ideals, I myself must have the same high ideals.

If in the past my friends and associates have not been a pleasure, perhaps I need to look deeply within my own self.

Do I use my friends for boosting my own ego? Do I look upon others as a means to success? Am I critical of others? Am I prejudiced? Am I an interested and faithful friend myself?

I evaluate myself fairly and honestly, for if I do not, I only cheat myself.

As I hold to high standards, as I am a true friend, I can know that companions of like mind will come into my world.

I give thanks for friends and for my own ability to be a friend.

When The Need Is To Stand Firm

I have taken a stand after long and prayerful meditation, and now there are those who would have me topple over.

I know that I must be strong, not merely stubborn. Even though voices all around me may plead for a change of heart — may point out the "unreasonable" ways of my decision — may in fact even rock me to and fro — my feet remain planted firmly in truth. My strength is not my own but from the faith in good within me.

I never have the feeling of faltering — only the awareness of divine strength to carry me through that which is mine to do.

I am secure in the knowledge that my Father-God will give me the right answers to the questioning of the world. I am confident that the end result will be a blessing for all.

I am strength! Thank You, Father.

To Help Remedy That "Left Out" Feeling

"Everybody" is doing that which I do not wish to do. I do feel so alone in a worldly sort of way. I do feel "left out" — not one of the group.

Yet I am where I am today because of choices and decisions of the past. Why am I in this particular group now?

Whatever the reason, it now comes to me as to how I may use this association for a blessing. It may be a test for my own courage. It most probably is to let my light shine for "someone" around that is seeking truth — though I may never know who.

I do not seek to display my differences of opinion from this group. I try to see our likenesses instead. I am quietly, yet confidently, my true self.

I give thanks that I may be a channel for truth. If I can be a blessing for another, I know that I myself will be blessed most of all.

For Times Of Anger

I am still. I breathe the breath of pure life. I hold each breath a moment and give thanks for life.

Life is too precious to waste in angry feelings and resentment.

I remember what the poisons of hatred can do to my body. Hatred burns down my body temple in the same manner that a raging fire might destroy a beautiful museum or a place of reverence.

Nothing in the outer world is worth harming my wondrous body temple that has served me so faithfully, and I release all adverse feelings here and now.

Whatever needs to be dealt with can be handled in wisdom and good judgment. I declare divine order in this situation.

With every breath I expel, anger leaves me. With every breath I draw, I become calm, and at peace.

For Times Of Tension

I relax in the presence of God. I feel the soothing, loving arms of Spirit holding me up above the shadow forms of confusion and conflict.

I reside in the real and the true. There is nothing but God — there is nothing but good, and all else is passing and temporary. How foolish I would be to put my faith and belief in the temporary! God's wisdom within swells up within my being and I know where to put my trust.

I believe in the good and everlasting. I believe in divine love. I believe in peace. I believe in divine order. I believe in myself as a divine spiritual being —free, secure, and in perfect harmony.

For Nonresistance

Though outer conditions may be filled with conflicts, I do not set up friction between the outer and my true inner nature. I do not speak words of negation, for they are against what I know is true for me. I will not act against the perfection which is in the center of my being.

Even as worldly rewards tempt me, I do not turn from truth which dwells within me. I will not enter into a personal war involving good and so-called evil. I know only good, and I stand strong.

Thank You, Father, for Your everlasting Presence within me that keeps me strong and secure. Thank You, Father, for insight and illumination as I approach every challenge of daily living.

When Tempted To Pass On "Interesting News"

I am in the "closet of my soul." Why do I need to tell this bit of information that has come my way? Is it to draw attention to myself? Is it to make me appear to be "in-the-know?" Is it possibly an acceptable way of getting back at another? Could it be spurred by a trace of resentment?

The answers to these questions come to me now and I know what to do. I know in my heart whether this bit of very "interesting news" is just that or whether it is in any way detrimental to myself or any other. I give thanks for light always as I now endeavor to be a pure channel for good only.

When Afraid Of The Future

I know that there is only one time in reality and that time is always *now*. I cannot relive yesterday, nor can I live tomorrow at this moment.

I cast aside all "problems" that I fear may mar my future, and I realize that my future is the offspring of my present state of consciousness.

For a perfect future, free from unhappiness and limitation, I must perfect my words, feelings, and actions now.

The only true insurance I can take out for the future is paid for right now by love, faith, goodwill, cheerfulness, honesty, and at-onement with my Creator-God.

I will pay the premiums, and I need never fear any thing or any one. Fear has no place in my life. I am a part of God, and therefore a part of all that is good.

To Help Attain Inner Calm In The Midst Of Nosiy Confusion

The sounds that are disturbing to me have no more power to upset or distract me, because I now take that power from them.

I go deep, deep down in the pool of my inner self. I hear only the music of my own heart — the rhythm of breathing — the joyful chimes of gladness for life.

To another these outer noises may mark occasions for rejoicing so I bless the occasion and all of those involved.

I bless the constant quietness that lies within me. I give thanks for my ability to commune with my Creator during any time and at any place.

I am calm as I rise from my inner pool and continue to float in the awareness of perfect peace.

For Locating A New Home

There is a perfect right home for me — right in every way. It is neither too large nor too small. It is convenient to my right work. It is located in the center of "my world" — the part of the world to which I am to minister at this particular time.

The walls of my new home are as expectant arms of a loved one awaiting my arrival.

I must learn where to go to find my home, so I now open my mind and my outer senses. I am alert and eager.

I give thanks, Father, for bringing me and my right home together. I hereby dedicate it as a sanctuary for spiritual learning and growth. May it be an oasis of peace and comfort to all who enter it.

When Making A Decision

I am filled with the power of perfect judgment. I am wise and true. I do not let another sway me or dictate to me what to do — even though I may be personally impressed with his good judgment.

I must seek the right answer for myself. Though solutions may often be similar for those with similar "problems" — just as every fingerprint differs, so do our needs. Therefore, I realize the importance of going within and finding my own special answer. It is there — for God, the answer to all, is there!

I give thanks for the right answer — the decision that will bring forth good in my life. And I give thanks for the courage to carry out the necessary steps leading to success, once my decision is reached.

To Help Eradicate Fear

God is here. I hold to this thought. There is no real power outside of God. Yet I have given something or someone a false, temporary power over me — otherwise I would not be afraid.

I now withdraw all false power, just as I would let air escape from a balloon. Though a "monster" toy balloon may loom over me, casting a shadow and appearing to be what it is not, without air it will collapse in a withered heap.

My old fear, empty of the power with which I had filled it, now lies inert and withered. *No* longer can it cast a shadow over my life and affairs.

Help me to know, Father, that You are the only power there is. With only good in power, what is there to fear?

To Call Forth Vitality And Health

Every atom in my body awakens fully as I speak these words: "You are filled with light. You are life. You are intelligent. You rejoice in knowing this truth."

I would not keep the atoms of my body prisoners of negation through my negative thoughts, words, and feelings. I love my wonderful body temple, and I set it free to enjoy its natural state of being.

My body was created as a vehicle for God expression. As I let every atom of my body know of its true mission, there is rejoicing and release.

My body happily responds to my commands, and the result is a freedom from all tensions and disease and a perfect fulfillment of wholeness. I am grateful.

For Release From
The Personal Will Of Another

I do not need to become angry. I do not need to entirely avoid this one that would dominate me. I certainly do not need to feel guilty. I only need to realize that I am a free spiritual being. My mind is always free to think the thoughts that I choose.

All annoying words from this person are instantly dissolved by divine love. I do not allow any irritating feeling to stay in my consciousness. This person can do absolutely nothing to me unless I allow him to.

I bless this one that must have some sort of emptiness in his own life — else there would be no desire to dominate another. I pray for his illumination and for the fulfillment of his needs.

I give thanks that I have dominion over all of my affairs. It is done unto me according to my own beliefs. Thank You, Father.

To Help Free One From The Urge To Dominate Another

The answer seems so clear to me. Why can't this one whom I would help see as I see?

Let me accept the truth, Father, that no other person in the universe has my consciousness — nor have I the consciousness of another. Though we are one in Spirit, yet each of us has been to a different spiritual school — has had different experiences — and thus reacts in different ways.

Perhaps I have the courage to face a situation in a particular manner with success. Another may not have the background that I have and may need to handle the situation in an entirely different manner.

I can swim; others have not learned how yet. Others ride bicycles in the park, while I walk. I express myself through talents and abilities that are unique to me. I must allow others to do the same.

Lift from me, Father, this urge to dominate a loved one. I pray only for his own illumination and for divine order to take place in his life.

To Aid In Job Success

Thank You, God, for Your activity in and through me as I seek to do Your work.

All work is divine. I see my work as an opportunity to express the divinity within me.

I do not ask that the "boss" be impressed, or that I be favored over any other worker, but rather that my work — my own special work — be so dedicated to bringing forth good for all that it cannot fail.

Inspire me, Father, to fulfill my part of Your great plan for me, so that all people everywhere may be blessed by the work that I do. As my work goes out to bless others, it must first of all move through and bless me. I give thanks for success.

To Use In Preparing A Garden

It takes a great deal of faith to plant tiny seeds and know that vines, plants, and bushes — big and small — bearing all kinds of melons, berries, and vegetables will in time appear.

Let me realize that God dwells in each tiny seed that I plant. God is in the rich soil, the sunshine, the rain.

It may occur to me that perhaps God does not even need me to tend the garden at all — yet I know that I was given dominion by God. I am needed to keep it safe and free from undergrowth. It is through my love and wisdom in caring for my garden that it will flourish fully. Every leaf and blossom will respond to my thoughts and touch.

I am filled with joy as I undertake to tend my garden. It will truly glorify God.

When Feeling Personally Responsible For Another

When my personal mind asks: "How will this one survive without me?" I know that I am off the path of truth. We are all in the care of our Father-Mother God and that is sufficient!

"How indeed did anyone get along without me from the very beginning of creation?" I must ask myself. "How has this one that I fear for now come this far?"

I realize how foolish I have been to think that it is up to me personally to protect and grow for another.

Father, help me to release this one to Your infinite care right now. You that created him can certainly care for him better than I. I accept my only true responsibility and that is to love this one and see him as Your child throughout eternity.

When Taking A Trip

First of all, I give thanks for this trip, Father. I give thanks for the many opportunities that it offers to meet new people and to see more of my beautiful earth home.

I give thanks that I am traveling in the protection of divine light — for the awareness that no matter where I go, I am ever in that light and no harm can befall me.

Make me deaf, Father, to any words of worry or pessimism concerning this trip. I simply will not hear them. I know that I am traveling in the aura of Your divine love and this is sufficient.

I give thanks for the privilege of being Your ambassador of peace as I travel through the land — not only by what I may say, but also by my actions. Therefore, I ask for a gentle reminder if I grow cranky or impatient with any one that serves me or if I forget to be my highest best self at any time.

Bless this trip, Father.

When My Plans Fail

I will not let my disappointment rob me of my faith. My faith is in good. Even though my plan seemed to be very good — to be just the right thing — evidently it is not the highest and best for me now.

Rather than blaming God for "letting me down," I thank God for insight and illumination to see why some other way is wiser for me.

Perhaps I need more preparation; if so, I am ready. Perhaps I need to complete something before this plan can really be beneficial to me or anyone else. If so, I will stay at the task in faith. Or it may be that I have aimed too low —that there is a higher call for me. If so, Father, I am listening; I am open; I am Yours.

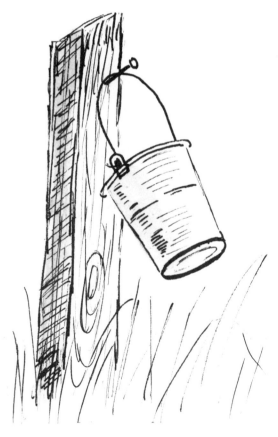

When A Loved One Passes On

I would not imprison my soul in the narrow walls of grief. There is no need for grief, for I have not lost anything in truth. All of the love that existed between us, dear one, is still active. All of the good that I brought out in you and all that you called forth in me lives forever.

Though we cannot touch hands in this change, we are ever touching in Spirit.

I would not hold you back any more than I would have prevented you from sailing to another shore while of this earth. In my mind, you are off to a wonderful new adventure in living.

I give thanks that my life was enriched by our shared experiences here. We will share experiences again — of that I am sure.

I now free you to God's loving care.

When A Change Is Needed

I know that there is some change needed in my life and affairs, Father, for I feel so dissatisfied and unfulfilled. I need to get out of this rut. It is pleasant in some ways — it is easy enough, I do not feel challenged any longer — I am performing by rote. My rut is worn smooth and well, and while I am bored, yet there is a certain amount of security in the known.

Give me even greater security in Your love, Father, so that I may lift myself from this place into another that needs my built-up experiences and my confidence. All life is growth and perhaps I feel unfulfilled because I have no more room in which to grow in this present situation.

Use me, Father, wherever I am needed to expand Your kingdom in some way. I give thanks for my new right place, which will add excitement, joy, enthusiasm, and greater meaning to my life.

Upon Awaking

I behold a fresh new day. Never for a moment did I doubt its birth, for I do have faith in divine order.

Let me be just as sure in knowing, Father, that there is good in this day...that there is beauty present which my eyes have yet to see — opportunities that could change my life entirely if I choose to accept them, delightful people in this day to whom I may have been blind in days past.

Truly awaken me this morning, Father, to this new and glorious day. Help me be alert through all my waking hours — not only to the outer, but also to the awareness of Your presence within.

Upon Going To Sleep

As I relax and ready myself for sleep, I feel no need to "count sheep." Rather, I visualize every little care of the day "jumping over the fence" and into my Father's keeping.

I let go of every physical tension, and pull up the spiritual blanket of divine protection — knowing that as I sleep, no harm can befall me.

I wish for myself happy and peaceful dreams. If there is a condition in the outer that has puzzled me, I ask for clear vision upon awakening. If there is a healing need in my body temple, I now put the healing power of God to work as I rest.

I look upon the darkness as a friend. The night has its own unique song that lulls and comforts. I am grateful for this time of rest, and I am grateful for sleep that refreshes and renews.

When Buying A Car

Thank You, Father, for all cars that give us such freedom in traveling and save us so much time. Thank You, too, for the superhighways, and also for the narrow country lanes over which I can travel.

As I choose a particular car for myself, I ask for guidance in using my judgment and will. I have an idea of what would meet my needs, yet I am always open to something better.

I bless the salesmen and the companies I meet as I shop for this car. I decree perfect understanding as we communicate.

My car is a blessing for me. It adds convenience and joy to my life. I drive as a child of God — with courtesy, consideration, good judgment, and wisdom.

Bless my new car, Father, and thank You.

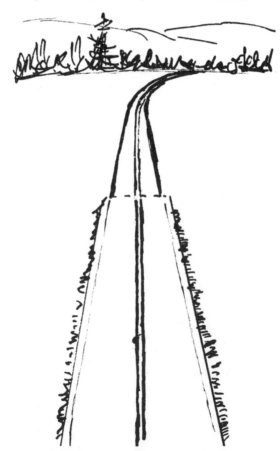

To Help Erase
An Unpleasant Dream

Dreams seem so real at times that they do affect our feelings. Realizing that this is so, I know that I cannot allow myself to become upset over a dream. It came as a result of some long-buried thought, perhaps, and I should be glad that my consciousness is now rid of it. Therefore I bless it and release it forever!

I know that God is all and God is good. Any nightmare that may come to haunt my waking hours is but a shadow. I chase it away with the power of light. I dwell in light, and consequently I have absolutely nothing to fear.

My mind is filled with thoughts of joy. My heart is filled with love.

To Help Quiet The Pangs Of Envy

My so-called competitor has won — has gained success. But this cannot mean that there is no more success available for anyone else. Because one flower blooms, this does not mean that there is no more sunshine, rain, and fertile soil to help another bloom.

I rejoice in the good that has come to another, for I know that there will always be unlimited good for all. If good has come to someone else, it can surely visit me too!

I release all thoughts of covetousness. What another has would never make me happy, for it is not mine. Perhaps I wish for similar good, yet it must not be borrowed from another. My own good is what I need and desire.

I give thanks for the good that has come to another. I give thanks for the good that is coming to me even now.

Before Writing
An Important Letter

My consciousness is emptied of all "stock phrases" and meaningless, overused words of formality. My mind is open to receive God-Mind, and I know exactly what needs to be made clear in this letter.

I can be sure that the letter conveys its message perfectly as I bless the act of writing it. I realize that I am writing to another child of God. I would not attempt to embarrass, blame, or deal unfairly with this one. My goal is for understanding, right action, and divine order.

As I send this letter out, I am sending out something very real — for words and thoughts are alive. Whatever I send out will in time return to me, therefore, I am very careful. I choose words and thoughts of love, life, hope, justice, integrity, and good will.

Bless this letter, Father, as it goes forth to touch the life of another.

Before Visiting The Sick

If I cannot help this one in the bondage of sickness, it is better that I stay away. I cannot sympathize in any manner —for this would only strengthen the chains that now bind the patient. I cannot afford to see him as he appears to be, for this is a false picture. I must see this one whole and free, as he is in the eyes of God. I must let him know in my manner and by my words that I consider him whole underneath this costume of infirmity.

Father, make me a channel of Your healing love as I visit this one today. Radiate through me the awareness of perfect life. Stir up a will to overcome in this one held down by lack of health ideas.

Keep me firm and sure in the awareness of truth as I look upon outer appearances.

Before A Family Reunion

Help me to realize, Father, that all members of the family are first of all Your heirs. Let me see each one as he truly is, instead of as I may have seen him in the past.

Sometimes it seems easier to be loving and understanding to strangers than to family, for we are not emotionally involved with strangers. Oh, Father, let me not be blinded to truth by my emotions! Help me to see each one at this family gathering as You see him.

Fill my heart with Your divine love, Father, that You may express through me and send out messages of harmony, goodwill and understanding.

Bless this reunion of family members — this gathering of free spiritual beings!

Before Praying For Another

Before I pray, I must be absolutely sure that I am not using prayer as a means to try to gain domination over another.

God is integrity, so it is impossible for me to dominate another through prayer. Have I ever prayed for a certain person to do a certain thing? Why? Almost always I can find the answer in a selfish reason. If I am lonesome, I must not pray for a specific person to visit, for that might not suit that person at this time. I have no right to involve this other person in anything unless he or she is willing. If I am lonesome, I must pray for my own fulfillment. If I am unhappy, I must not pray for someone to bring happiness to me by performing a certain act. I must know that true happiness lies within myself.

As I pray for others, let me ever be aware, Father, that the only right I have is to pray for their highest good. When I hold another in Your light, his life will be blessed in the right way — in turn blessing mine.

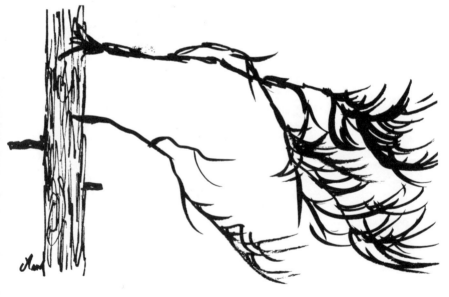

When Giving A Gift

As I give this material gift, let me be aware of what I can truly give *through* this gift.

I can give joy. Joy within is stirred up and called forth by sharing. I can give a sense of worthiness to another through this gift. (We do not give gifts to the unworthy, do we?) Most of all, I can give love. Long after the gift is used up, worn out, or misplaced, the love that was given through it remains. Not only does love remain, but it multiplies and in turn is given out to others.

No matter what gift I give, let me give it in love. It is really the love involved that makes glad the heart of the receiver.

It is a privilege to be a gift-bearer. Father-God, clear from my consciousness any motive other than pure love as I give this gift.

For One's Birthday

My birthday is a time for measuring growth and recording results. It is my very own special day for rejoicing in life, love, health, and harmony.

I ponder these questions today:

Am I as enthusiastic about life as I was on my last birthday?

Am I moving toward some desired and purposeful goal?

Am I practicing good spiritual health habits, as well as good physical health habits?

Am I willing to change?

Am I feeling older instead of more spiritually mature?

Father, if I am off the lighted path, I ask Your assistance, Your divine guidance. I know that I was not created merely to mark time upon this earth plane. Help me to realize that even though circumstances do change, each year of life is to increase in hope, enthusiasm, and joyful service.

Right now, on my birthday, I begin a new year of spiritual expansion!

For A Rainy Day

I give thanks for this rainy day. Perhaps it cancelled some picnics and boating parties, emptied parks and caused children to spend the day indoors — yet I see the leaves refreshed and cool. I see grass already greener, rivers swelling, housetops shiny clean!

Thank You, God, for rainy days — for these remind me that I too, from time to time, need "rainy days" within. I need a time to refresh my soul. I need a time for cleansing myself from the dust of worldly negativity. I need to replenish the river of life within.

Bless this rainy day, Father, and bless my own periods of cleansing and refreshment. Just as the flowers of the earth burst into bloom and emit their fragrance for all to enjoy after the nourishment of rain, sun, and soil — so do I unfold and give to my world as I turn regularly to inner nourishment.

To Use Before Shopping

There is in my Father's storehouse, that which meets my need exactly and as I go out to find it I am confident and relaxed.

I give thanks for good judgment with which to make wise choices. I am not swayed by the words of others, but I listen within and make a choice that will be a blessing to me.

Although there is unlimited good for me, I am not greedy. I would not drink a gallon of lemonade when a glass is sufficient. On the other hand, there is no need for fearful self-denial.

Thank You, Father, for the right purchase which is right for me in every way.

Upon The Reality Of God

I do not have to argue with another to establish the reality of God. I do not have to cling to a blind faith. *I know.* I know God is because I am. I feel my heart beat, and I feel God. I see myself doing the right thing — taking the right action — and in this vision I see God. I hear God in every word of truth. I believe in God because by turning my mind and heart to thoughts of wholeness and good, my attitudes and experiences change. They change by the mighty, sweeping power of Spirit. If there were no God, there could be no change.

The power of God is more real to me than any outer condition. The power of God has worked miracles and continues to work miracles. It has changed fear into faith — despair into joy — failure into success — hate into love —disease into wholeness — disbelief into sure knowing. I know my God to be a living, moving power for good, and I take time to glorify and praise Him.

Upon My Own Being

Why am I here? Where have I been? What is my purpose in being on earth? If I still myself and listen within, I will gain insight. I will know that there is but one period of time for me; the present. I cease blaming past conditions, because I chose them. I chose them by my thoughts, words, and feelings. In truth, I am where I am right now as a direct result of my thoughts, words, and feelings.

What is my purpose in being on earth? It is to develop my soul, to learn, to grow. I am privileged to be enrolled in this earth school. I have the finest of schoolmasters — the Christ Mind within me. I have a beautiful laboratory in which to work, classmates who help me with my lessons, clearcut rules to follow, yet it is all up to me. Only through desire for good in my life, followed by determination to practice and keep spiritual law, do I move ahead.

I am. I am here. I thrill to the joy of being.

When All Is Well

All is well in my world, Father, and I give thanks. Help me to realize fully that this state of bliss did not happen accidentally. It happened as a result of my faith in good. My heaven is always present, just a thought away. It is mine at any time that I can rest completely in truth, knowing that I am one with all good, one with wholeness, one with perfect harmony.

I know that there are still higher rungs on my spiritual ladder, that I have many lessons to learn and challenges to meet; but I also know that all will continue to be well with me as long as I remember my oneness with You, Father.

The light that radiates from Your Spirit within me eliminates all shadows, all fears, all doubts.

All is well in my world, Father, for I am in Your care.

A Healing Meditation For The Feet

I walk in peace and understanding and I am healed. I am a light to all that I meet each day and I bless my feet that take me joyously on my way. With each step I take I say the word PEACE.

I take unnecessary burdens off my feet by releasing any thought or feeling that is not good and positive.

I walk in peace as I come to realize that God indwells all — every person and every thing.

My path is free and illumined as I look to God as my divine guide. I bless my feet now and dedicate them to the service of good.

A Healing Meditation For
The Stomach Area

I give thanks for divine wisdom within that enables me to choose wisely — the food I eat and the emotions that I store. I let go all thoughts and feelings of injustice. I know that in God there is absolute justice. I cease finding fault with myself as well as with others. I concentrate on the good present in each living soul.

I live in the golden circle of God's perfect love. I am loved. I am secure. I am at peace with all. I know that God is the divine adjuster — everywhere present. I know that all things work together for my highest good as I trust the divine law in all things.

I give thanks for good judgment present within me now.

A Healing Meditation For The Heart And Lung Area

I am free in the freedom of Divine Love. Divine Love does not dominate the beloved, but gently frees and blesses always. Divine Love is not possessive, but realizes the truth that we are all one in Spirit.

God dwells in every human soul, therefore, I can have no enemies. My only real enemies are my own negative thoughts and feelings. I realize them now — one by one.

Love is harmonizing me now. Love is freeing me. Love is balancing my life. God is loving His world through me and I rise up whole and free.

Thank You, Father.

A Meditation To Use
Before Surgery

God's hands are all around me. My surgeon's hands are God's hands as they repair my body temple. The hands of all the nurses that minister unto me are instruments of kindness and loving service. The hands that make my bed and clean the floor are good hands — therefore, God's hands.

I bless them every one and now relax in the knowledge that God is working through every soul that I encounter in this experience.

I am in His loving care and keeping. There is no room for fear in my heart, for it is filled completely with Divine Love.

Thank You, Father.

A Meditation For Calming
The Emotions

I am steadfast and unwavering in my faith in good. Only the good is true and eternal, for all else passes away.

I am in control of my thoughts and feelings, for my Creator has given me this privilege.

Knowing that my emotions are quick to respond to every thought and feeling I hold — I hold only thoughts and feelings of love, peace and goodwill. I release all thoughts and attitudes of bitterness, resentment and condemnation. Worry and anxiety depart as I place my confidence in the unfailing power of Spirit.

I am filled with peace. I am filled with poise. I am filled with joy.

A Meditation For After Surgery

The knitting needles of Spirit are now knitting together that which has been taken apart. I feel this restorative work of Spirit and I relax and surrender my entire being to it.

I release any thought of imperfection, for I know that in the mind of my Creator I am perfect and whole always.

I give thanks for the healing activity now taking place within. I give thanks for my wonderful body, and its ability to function perfectly. I give thanks for renewed strength and for renewed joy in living!

A Meditation For The Throat Area

Words are powerful. Every word that I speak makes a mark upon my body temple. Therefore, I do always endeavor to let the "words of my mouth and meditation of my heart" be of the highest nature.

I give thanks that all power has been given me to control my thoughts and to choose my words.

I refuse to voice criticism. I do not withhold words of love. I do not try to accept what is not pure and whole. Always I turn within and feel the flow of the Christ love for all people everywhere.

A Healing Meditation For The Back

God is my strength and my support. Whatever I am now supporting without love, I release, for it is not mine. Whatever I support in love is never a burden. Therefore, I gather all of my true responsibilities and obligations together and place them in Divine Light.

I feel no resentment toward anyone or any situation. I am perfectly balanced as I give and take in every area of living.

I am free from burdens. I am free of resentments. I acknowledge the one and only power — God, the good.

I am a channel of perfect strength and freedom.

Thank You, Father.

A Healing Meditation For
The Eyes And Ears

I have faith in good and in the power of good. My eyes are illumined by thoughts of love, joy, peace, harmony and good will. I banish from my being all false thoughts and feelings of cruelty, selfishness, fear and suspicion.

My ears hear not only the joyous sounds around me, but they hear perfectly the inner voice of Spirit. I am obedient to the perfect guidance ever being given me. I am willing to be instructed in truth by the whole spirit of God.

I have faith in the spiritual power of my mind. My faith in good cleanses my eyes and my ears.

I see! I hear!

Thank You, Father.

A Healing Meditation For The Whole Body

I now release any image I am holding of myself as imperfect or diseased in any way. I am God's perfect child and I know it.

God created me and God knows how to correct that which is presently distorted or unbalanced. God is healing me now. God is filling my heart with His perfect love. God is expressing through me as life, strength, and peace.

I give thanks for perfect health in body and mind. Health is my inheritance from my Father God and I accept it in gratitude and joy.

A Blessing For One Who
Has Passed On

You are no longer present here in the body, dear one, and you are missed. But you are now where you are supposed to be — still loved and loving — still growing in spiritual awareness — ever a child of God.

I release you to enter this new realm freely and joyously. I would not bind you to this earth for selfish reasons. I bless you and see you surrounded by the light of love and illumination.

There is no death in Spirit. There is only life — and though that life stream may flow through many "lands," it is an eternal river.

I rejoice in the thoughts of life eternal, and I now send these thoughts to you, dear soul.

Blessing For The New Born Baby

Welcome little soul! You are in for a wonderful experience, for this time and this place is exactly right for you!

May you always be aware of the beauty around you — even in the mundane and seemingly ordinary.

May you be blessed with family and teachers that are not afraid to let you express yourself and follow your own star, but that will help and guide you along the way even when your special star seems small or dim to their eyes.

May you grow into the realization that you are God's child first of all, and are ever surrounded by His love, His peace and His protection.

Blessing For A Marriage

Bless the union of these two souls, Father, and help each to know the responsibilities involved. Help each to realize that a partner in marriage is not to be possessed or manipulated in any way, but rather freed to go out and bring back treasures for the two to share.

Let each one meet the other in love and understanding — never afraid to speak freely of deep desires, longings, fears or seeming problems.

May talents be developed in the rich soil of encouragement and patience.

May there always be the remembering that each is God's expression of love to the other, and a rejoicing in and for this love.

A Birthday Blessing For Another

Today is your special day and I behold you in the light of love, joy and peace. This is the day your soul chose from all the rest to begin this life's joyous expression of living.

A birthday marks the start of a new year — a time for releasing all the hurts and disappointments of the past year and a time for beginning again. Throughout this new year, may you experience the combination of love and wisdom in all of your experiences and affairs.

I light the candle of love for you. May you know the truth of your origin. You were created by divine love.

I light the candle of joy for you. May you feel within yourself that quiet enthusiasm that springs from within as we come to appreciate ourselves and others, as divine beings.

I light the candle of order for you. Knowing that order is heaven's first law, may you claim for yourself order in every aspect of life.

I light the candle of abundant health and prosperity for you. These are yours by your birthright as a child of God.

Happy Birthday!

PART III

Creative Meditation

Creative Meditation

You are about to enter through a magic door — the magic door of your mind! Imagination is the key and we all have an imagination. This technique of meditation is not only practical, but it is fun. The purpose, of course, is to change the subconscious mind.

Know one thing, however — *The subconscious mind is not fooled or tricked.* The subconscious mind gets the true message. If we secretly wish we could be sick for a day to avoid some unpleasant task, it obliges us. If we see things in shop windows that we would like, yet feed the thought of not being able to afford them into the subconscious mind, we can be sure the subconscious mind will keep us in a state of poverty. Never jokingly remark: "I could have died!"; or "That burned me up!"; or "He makes me sick!" Imagine the reaction of the body to these and other negative remarks.

Whatever you truly want to be, you can be *if* you can convince your subconscious mind of it.

A lovely and talented girl became crippled — bedridden. For years she lay helpless — being fed — being bathed and totally cared for by others. She constantly said, "I am going to walk again." She was very convincing to other people. She did not convince her subconscious mind, however. Perhaps this little story will tell us why:

One day her nurse had to leave the room for a few minutes. She was doing her daily leg exercises and her nurse instructed her to continue while she was out of the room. As the nurse passed by the outside window of her patient's room, she lovingly peeked back through a disheveled venetian blind only to discover that her patient lay still already. Why? She was puzzled and made it a point to leave several more times that week during exercise time. Each time she left, the patient stopped exercising instantly. She was living a lie. She did not really want to walk again and her subconscious mind got the message very clearly. For the subconscious mind records our thoughts and our emotions as well as our spoken words. We must be absolutely and totally committed to our desire in order to bring it forth.

After many unhappy years for many people, this beautiful, talented crippled girl came to realize the truth about herself. She was filled with fear. She was afraid of life. She was afraid of competition. She was afraid she could not hold her husband as a normal person. After coming to this realization and ridding herself of these false fears — she did walk again.

Your "true self" — that self in you that is happy, healthy, wise, prosperous, and well-adjusted — is struggling to express itself. If you are not happy, healthy, rich and successful, you are living a lie! You are being something other than your true self! Your conscious mind has made a prisoner of your true self by accepting untrue remarks and attitudes offered by the world. It is your job to instruct your conscious mind to unlock the prison door and allow your true self freedom.

Suppose You Don't Know What You Want To Be

You do know. That "true you" at the center of your being knows exactly what you really are, and therefore what you yearn to express and be.

"Well, then, why don't I know right now?" you may ask, and with good reason. The reason you don't realize your true yearnings at the moment is due to a good job of camouflage — inner camouflage. The first bit of cover-up work may have been done while you were just a tiny baby resting securely in your mother's arms, by remarks such as these made by loving relatives and friends:

"My, my, doesn't that nose look just like Uncle Henry's. You'd better watch this one, my dear!" (Exclaimed in jest, of course.)

"An Anderson right down the line!" (Meaning any number of things!)

"Oh, I can see it now — a real heartbreaker in the next generation."

etc.

etc.

etc.

Then came larger "leaves" of camouflage which were placed exactly on the spot — further removing your "true self" from your awareness. If it did indeed appear to be a fact that you might be a heartbreaker, two things may have happened. Your parents, in fear, may have thoroughly convinced you that sex is bad, the opposite sex is not to be trusted, and it is sinful, sinful, sinful to play the role of a heartbreaker. Or, on the other hand, they may simply have given in to the suggestion and actually paved the way, unconsciously, of course, for you to become the great heartbreaker of all time. But either way, *don't blame your parents!* Always remember one thing — parents always do the very best that they are capable of at the time. No one can do better, but if we see that we need to undo something that was innocently done by our parents or grandparents, we should do it without guilt. The damage was done without malice and it should be undone without guilt.

The next step is the actual undoing of these false notions about ourselves. This is not always easy, for we want the approval of those that are near and dear to us. We don't want to separate ourselves from the only security we know.

Let us consider the case of Henry J. Marshmallow. Henry J. was the apple of Mother's eye. He had been told repeatedly by doting relatives that he was just like Mother. Henry J. took on Mother's mannerisms, opinions and habits. As he grew into manhood (?) Henry J. became Mother's constant and most attentive companion. While Henry J. appeared to enjoy the constant round of visiting and vacationing with Mother, his "true self" that yearned to express its individuality, shrank and dimmed — yet that tiny light of hope and truth never *completely* goes out!

Nor is the light completely out for Amy Aimless — sweet, demure and wishy-washy. Amy is wishy-washy simply because she wishes to wash one way and she is expected to wash another! She is standing, emotionally, in the middle of life's seesaw — watching others go up and down — hearing others squealing with the delights and expectations of living. Amy is not truly living, for she is not going anywhere — she cannot move, for her desires are pulling her one way and the desires others have for her are pulling her just as strongly in another direction! Yet Amy feels that she cannot do what she wants to do. If she does, others may be disappointed in her — her image would be broken and some people would miss that particular image! Do you know Amy Aimless?

One of the most courageous men I know shared his own "moment of hopelessness" with me. Many years ago before his courage had come forth, he related how he gazed out the window of his impressive home, watching the blackbirds peck around for an early morning meal. More burdens lay on his shoulders than he could possibly live with he thought. Although he had left home at an early age and had no formal education past the fifth grade in public school, he had managed to elevate himself to a high position in a large company. Indeed, it was his "true self" that propelled him away from the scene of utter poverty and ignorance. It was his "true self" that gave him the stamina to study on his own time — to take whatever opportunity — whatever job came to him to do. His "true self" took him so far without any question it seems, simply because he was free to be himself. His family did not appear to care one way or the other how he fared. He had no one to answer to. He was his own man and thus a delight to his "true self." Then he came to the rock wall. The bride of his youth had turned into a selfish, demanding woman. Through the years, he had quite innocently allowed himself to become enslaved by her wishes and demands. She wanted no social life, no further study (for him), no outside interests (for either of them) — only his paycheck and his fidelity. He tried to reason with her. He wanted more in marriage than this. His "true self" wanted more than this. But his nose rested against the proverbial wall. His grown children frowned upon his even considering going against their mother's wishes. What would the church say about the divorce he was thinking about? What would happen to his political career?

All of these thoughts surrounded him as he watched the flock of blackbirds move as one across his carefully manicured lawn. Suddenly a hawk came from nowhere it seemed and dove upon one single blackbird. The others scattered, leaving the unfortunate one helpless, in the strong grip of the hawk. As this man stood watching and listening to the desperate squawks of the blackbird, he felt only empathy. He *was* that blackbird — hopelessly trapped. His "true self was dying — or so he thought. He turned from the window —sick and cold.

But life is not snuffed out that easily. The "hawks" of this world cannot capture all of the blackbirds. Life is the winner always. Life came to the aid of this man during his time of hopelessness and gave him the yearning to live — to truly *live*. Life said to him as he went through the paces of working — eating — bathing — dressing — "You are not a blackbird. You are not a slave to another. You have a mind —a mind so special that no one can think your thoughts for you or make decisions for you. *You* are in control of your own mind."

As time went on this man freed himself a bit more. He began to see himself as an individual of some worth. He began to think of himself as a creative being — creative because he was able to use his mind. First came the question, "Can I change things?" Then came the answer, "You must!"

And he did. After the life forces were stirred up within him, Life itself rushed to save him. Opportunities came to him — people reached out to inspire him — he became involved in living — and he prayed.

Recently he related, "I feel as if the trapped blackbird

within me gained super-strength, threw off the hawk and is now fully recovered from his wounds. Life is great!"

We all have "hawks" to attack us at sometime in life, and we either succumb or gain the super-strength needed to break away. How we react to the "hawks" that would destroy us depends upon one thing. That is our *desire* for something better — for good in our life.

You are probably thinking: "Well, don't we all want good in our life?" Yes, of course we do! But here is where "the haves" and "the have-nots" are separated. The world is full of people wishing for everything the mind can imagine — people looking out of windows, wishing and waiting and waiting and waiting. There are the obese — wishing that they were slim and all the while eating more than their body needs. There are those in inharmonious situations — wishing for peace and quiet — yet adding to the fires of condemnation and confusion. It is one thing to wish and quite another to realize a deep desire. Wishes flit through our minds all day. A desire is persistent — it is born of a true need and grows as it is nurtured by our encouragement.

A deep desire grown to maturity has changeability. Any thing — any condition — any situation in our life can be changed by a true desire for change.

Desire is the prerequisite for membership in the *"See Me Be Club!"* We *see* the change — we envision it — dream of it — live it — even though it may be hard for us at first to believe that we are a part of it. Next, we manage to put self into the picture — *me*. Then simply relax and let it all *be*. You can *be* whatever you believe and *see* yourself being in your mind's eye. You know good happens to others. Ask yourself often, "Why not good for *me?*"

If you have a deep desire — be thankful for it. Good is on its way into your life. Nourish your desire. Join the "See Me Be Club." Begin to walk, to talk, to act out the role of that person that you wish to be — that in truth you already are! Spread your blackbird wings — throw off the hawk of limitation and rise up to new freedom of being.

There is a story of a woman who inherited a palace, yet

gave it up simply because it was too much bother for her to move. She had always wanted to live in the locale of the newly inherited palace. She had often lamented over the fact that she needed more room to do all of the things that she had never been able to do. She had fussed and complained about her shabby dwelling place — yet she couldn't give it up!

We all tend to be more or less like this to some degree. We hold on to our limitations and even our illnesses simply because we are in a familiar rut with them. They offer an alibi. They give us reason for not amounting to anything — or rather not being our "true self."

We sometimes fear change, yet nature is changing constantly. Perhaps the change itself is not always easy or pleasant, but good does come with change.

A friend and I were walking the beach after a storm. I was finding the most beautiful beach treasures and remarked that these were the loveliest I had ever found.

"That was the worst storm we have ever had!" my friend answered. "These treasures were brought from the very bowels of the sea."

Can you imagine what might be hidden in the "bowels" of your being? Perhaps great courage, love, genius, and unimagined good! What kind of storm would it take to bring them forth?

Yet we do not need to go through a storm in order to realize the good within. However, often times we do need some sort of "shaking up" before we will reach down within our "true self" and find our own special treasures.

One of the most beautiful souls I am privileged to know was once a most arrogant, spoiled and selfish person. Her only daughter was mangled and mutilated in a tragic freak accident. She is still in an institution — constantly begging for her mother to come to her. As if that were not enough to cope with, she went through a marital split and then a great financial loss. Of course, she could have grown into a mature loving person without these difficulties, but she must be admired because during these periods, she did reach down into the "bowels of her being," so to speak, and bring forth the gifts of her true beautiful self.

Why Do We Make Unwise Choices In The First Place?

"Nothing in my life is right — absolutely nothing!" lamented an elderly acquaintance. She went on to talk about her wish for death, yet I became more and more aware of her longing for good and longing for life. She was totally frustrated.

"How did I get into this hell?" she kept asking.

How indeed? How do any one of us get into the "hell" that we find ourselves in from time to time? Almost without exception we can trace it back to an unwise choice, and almost without exception we can trace that unwise choice directly to a fear. Fear is a destroyer. Fear is the largest hawk that we must escape from and rise above.

This unfortunate trapped woman must have been a spoiled child by all reports. Spoiled children are almost always lacking in self-respect and self-confidence, for they have not had the opportunity to prove themselves as individuals. Spoiled children simply rely upon their parents to provide them with their needs and wishes. Fear that their human parents may die or for some reason cease to provide them with what they want causes them to live with a restless fear.

As a young girl, this woman (whom we will call Ethel for the rest of this story) wanted marriage so badly that she was not wise in her choice of a husband. She picked a husband who was even weaker than she herself was. He had no job and no source of income, so Ethel feathered their nest with her parents' furniture and money. Why did Ethel make this move? Simply from fear — fear that she would be unable to marry, otherwise.

In a short time, young Ethel and her groom were living in the home with Ethel's parents and eventually, Ethel's father turned over his business to his son-in-law, in order to satisfy his only daughter.

A child was born, named after Ethel's father, and the little family group appeared to be happy — until Ethel's suspicions were verified and she was certain that her husband was having an affair. Again fear clutched her and she refused to admit the truth. Her parents must never know. Her doctor must never know. Above all, her friends and neighbors must never know. But in her secret dark world, Ethel brooded and grew into a real shrew. She never missed an opportunity to put her husband down — to make him feel small and worthless — to hurt him back for hurting her. Her only son somehow survived a childhood filled with hostility and resentment and left home as soon as he reached adulthood. Ethel's parents died shortly after the final departure of her son.

Ethel's one remaining joy in life after this was entertaining, but the time soon came when Ethel and her husband lost the property which had been left them, due to Ethel's unwise spending.

Fear attracts more fear, and by now Ethel had a mountain made of fear. Fear that her son truly hated her — fear that her husband would embarrass her in her circle of friends — fear that she would have to live on welfare — fear that she would die unloved.

Ethel, in her old age, was a pitiful, broken soul. She forgot how to smile.

Is it too late for Ethel to find peace? Certainly not, but she must *desire* it with all her soul and mind. And she must believe it possible.

At this point, however, Ethel has not reached the pinnacle of deep *desire* necessary for change. She cannot admit her unwise choices. She is fighting back with the old hawk of confusion, blow for blow — round after round after round. She is wearing herself out — unaware that she could make a break and move up above the level of confusion.

When Ethel wants "out" badly enough, Life will answer her call. Until that time she might be heard arguing with herself in this manner: "It isn't fair!"; "It's not my fault!"; "How could he treat me that way?"; I never wronged anybody!"; "It isn't fair!"

Ethel continues to ask for guidance. Someday she will be able to guide herself out of this misery, hopefully.

* * *

The world has coined such phrases as, "Poor, but honest" and "Poor, but happy" and most people have bought them. What a pity! We were never meant to be poor. In truth, it is a sin to be poor, for we are not expressing our true self in poverty.

Think of all the sins committed in the world which stem directly from poverty and lack.

Larry G. was on his way up. He became assistant manager for a large chain grocery store. He bought a modest home for his wife and three small children and all was well until his wife became desperately ill. Hospital bills claimed all of Larry G.'s savings and ate into his weekly income. He became further and further in debt until there simply was not enough to meet the daily needs of living. They sold the luxuries and tried to hold onto the essentials, but even so things were too tight.

Larry G. was headed for a nervous breakdown as he watched his family do without. His children grew pale and drawn before his very eyes as they were deprived of the very food which he worked in every day.

With great resentment and hostility Larry G. began stealing fresh fruits and meats from the store for his family. He told them that they were "bargains," but he himself could not touch them! In fact, in a very short time Larry G. could only eat oatmeal and milk. His actions made him sick.

At this point, Larry G. gave up. He cried out for help and help came. Through counseling, he began to see the truth and understand the laws of the universe. He learned how to convince his subconscious mind that he was worthy of riches and he became rich in many ways.

During her illness, his wife had been developing a latent talent for oil painting and she began to sell her works of art.

An old business partner of Larry G.'s uncle tracked him down in order to pay off a debt which had bothered him for a year. And Larry G. himself was made a manager of a brand-new store after making a clean breast of matters with his bosses. They were impressed with his endurance and with his integrity — and even more with his new-found confidence.

What Larry G. really possessed was his new-found true self, which made him realize that in order to serve others best we *need* to be healthy, happy and wealthy. Poverty is a devil — a devil hawk that must be overcome.

*   *   *

Louise learned early in life that it was easier to outwardly agree with the authority — namely her parents. But how Louise seethed inwardly! She became completely passive — catering to her dominant parents every suggestion and wish. And she also became very emotionally ill.

What actually brought Louise to seek help was the fact that she did not want to bear a child after six years of marriage. She was perfectly willing to adopt a child, but she did not want one of her own flesh and blood.

When Louise learned the truth behind her outer reasoning, she was shocked. Louise did not want a child of her own simply because she unconsciously hated her parents and the husband they had guided her to marry. She rebelled at being the channel through which their grandchild and child would come. She was struggling for her freedom.

Louise first had to learn that she must love herself. She hated herself most of all for being weak.

Louise learned to respect herself as a unique being — a creation of the Divine. She realized that she did not belong to her parents — and not even to her husband — but to life itself. She had a reason for being. She was a soul. She had lessons to learn. She had a right to happiness!

Louise decided to separate herself from her husband and her parents for awhile. She decided to study herself — to study life. She had preferences — which she learned to respect and act upon. Louise found herself. She liked herself and she was happy living alone.

However, Louise realized that she must be strong enough to face her family, otherwise, she would merely be living a fantasy. Louise did face them, and was surprised to find that her parents respected her. They had to! Self-respect demands respect from others. Louise took a second look at her husband. Her parents had chosen a good stable husband for her, she realized. They decided to work things out and build a life together based on respect for each other and freedom to express.

* * *

This final case history which I feel led to share with you is by far the most dramatic and inspiring. It truly shows just what can be done when the desire for good is strong enough.

I met Jolene one hot summer day in an apartment complex. My phone was out of order and I went across the hall and tapped lightly on the door. Most of the apartment dwellers worked during the day, but somehow I sensed a presence. As I knocked I became aware of moaning and sobbing on the other side of the door. No one came. I finally left, but could not forget the pathetic sobs and once again went to the door, tapping lightly. I had the feeling that I was blocked out by some overwhelming grief and bravely I turned the door knob.

There on the floor of an absolutely bare apartment sprawled the form of a woman. After a moment, I realized that she was hovering over something — was it an animal or a small child. She moved and revealed its identity — a typewriter!

We looked at each other for a few moments — neither knowing what to say.

"Let me get us both a cup of hot coffee," I said, and hurried back to my apartment. I took my time in preparing a tray of coffee and buns and when I returned, my neighbor was at least sitting erect on the bare floor. I joined her.

"I want to use your phone," I explained. "Mine is out of order this morning."

Her eyes misted suddenly and she shook her head.

"I don't have a phone — yet," she replied in a low-pitched voice.

We sipped coffee quietly and steadily. No words were necessary, it seemed. After the coffee cups were emptied, I learned that her name was Jolene. She had moved in two days ago. She had left an unhappy marriage. Her family would not support her in her move. She was without money and without a job. All that she had was used to rent the apartment. She had an old station wagon with little gas in it parked out in the parking area.

"I was upset," she explained soberly, "because my one possession — my love — won't work!" She pointed to the typewriter. It was old, but had been quite an expensive typewriter, I could see. The cord went across the bare floor to the receptacle. I reached over and turned it on. It appeared to be "dead." But why?"

"I dropped it," Joline said as if to answer my unasked question.

"Flip the wall switch," I nearly commanded.

She did — and the typewriter hummed with joy! We laughed hysterically and talked the afternoon away. As Jolene went to the closet, I was relieved to see that she *did* have some clothes! She brought out a large chart filled with pictures cut from magazines and laid it out on the floor between us.

"These are the things I want," she said as she passed her hands over the chart. "I want a happy, peaceful dwelling — furnished!" she added laughing. "I want a job. I want time to write. I want friends. I want money. And I want to look like this!" She pointed to a picture on the chart of a beautiful, slim and confident woman about her age.

I looked at Jolene — obese, red-eyed, and broke. I looked at the emptiness of the apartment surrounding her and out the window at her dilapidated old station wagon.

She looked me squarely in the eyes and said, "If I cannot prove once and for all that I am a free-thinking being — not an animal or a robot — and can make my life what I want it to be — then I want to know it soon!"

Her eyes seemed to be riveted on an empty picture hook on the wall. She turned and once again dug into the treasures of her one closet, coming out with a sampler which bore these beautiful words, "For as he thinkest in his heart, so is he." (Prov. 23:7)

Jolene became almost unreal in a sense — yet more true and exciting than any personality I had ever known. The first thing I noticed was her normalization of body weight. She did not count calories, she did not even weigh herself —

yet she gradually over a period of time became the person in the picture on her chart. She told me that she thought of her body as a beautiful temple and she only ate what she thought would benefit it.

And I watched in amazement as the furniture vans came periodically to Jolene's apartment with some needed piece of furniture. Or Jolene would bring home a small piece herself that she had usually picked up, such as a real bargain at an antique sale.

One afternoon as we drank hot coffee and talked together, Jolene caught my gaze and laughed out loud. From my chair in the kitchenette I had a full view of all of her pocketbooks lined up across the dresser in her bedroom — all opened.

"That is my way of saying — I have need of some extra money. I'm ready to receive it!" she explained.

Several mornings later, Jolene waved two envelopes at me in passing and called out, "It's here! I sold an article and got a refund!" Another small miracle in the life of Jolene.

In all the years since Jolene has never stopped growing and miracles have never stopped happening. She became all she wanted to be and more — and so can you. Next we will talk about the door to success and how it can open up a new life for anyone that will faithfully use it.

* * *

The Theater Of Your Mind

The magic door of your mind actually opens into a wonderful theater — the director of which is your imagination. When we use the imagination to see our good we are using what I call "creative meditation." We create by constant and continuous thoughts and actions depicting that which we deeply desire.

The true desire for something better comes from our Creator, for we were not created to be slaves of circumstance. Each one of us has the potential to rise above any circumstance and express the divinity which was implanted in us in the beginning. Our Creator created creativity itself. We as heirs have the right to use this ability to create and bring forth our highest good.

Most times young children have less trouble using their gifts of imagination than do adults. The reason for this is, of course, that children have not lived long enough to have their true selves "buried" by fears, limitations and worldly opinions.

I have marveled at the results that I have obtained over the years by encouraging children to *be* what they want to be! In over twenty years of public school teachings, I have never had a child who believed he could read not learn to read! Sometimes my biggest hurdle has been to get a student to believe in himself.

For some reason we seem to have much more faith in others than we have in ourselves. Some times we even have more faith in other people's children, other people's parents, or other people's doctors, lawyers, etc. Why? Perhaps because the familiar seems so ordinary. Perhaps because we need to learn to love and respect ourselves more.

Many years ago my daughter, then about nine, badly needed some help in reading. She had been tutored for three years to no avail, it seemed. She had attended summer school and again no apparent progress. Being a teacher myself, I felt that if one person could help her, I could! But parents are often the very ones who cannot help. At this time I prayed for guidance — and it was quick to come. A vision of myself as another personality flashed across my mind — and that was the answer.

Dressed in a brown hat to cover my hair and an outfit unfamiliar to my daughter, I became "Mrs. Brown," her teacher for the summer. She never once failed to play the game and her progress was fantastic that summer!

Do you think it impossible to help yourself? Do you feel too familiar with yourself to trust yourself? Then you too may need to play a game.

* * *

Now let us set up a theater in our minds. Let us see on

the marquee our own name. Don't rush through this process, but pause and enjoy every part of it. Look at your name — caress each letter and think about this being your identity. Hear your name with your inner ear. Think deeply about your source — your true source. Know that each of us is first of all a child of the Creator with all of the benefits and rights that go with it. Look again at that name on the marquee of your mental theatre. That name is important!

Now you are inside. It is quiet and semi-dark. Find a seat and relax your body. Listen to the soft music that is being played in the background. Look up at the rich velvet curtains. Look around the theatre and note its beauty and richness. This is the finest, most elegant theatre that could ever be imagined!

The music fades. The curtain slowly opens and there on center stage is your true self — your self as you would like to be — poised, confident, healthy, wealthy and wise! You *are* that which you most want to be. You are doing that which you most want to do.

As the play ends, you applaud mentally and affirm, "Yes, that's the way it is!" As you leave the theater, you take on the qualities, mannerisms and personality of your true self. You and your true self are one!

Now, it is most important that you go back to this same theatre every day — preferably twice a day — and view this *very same play* in which your true self stars. The play *never* changes once it has been written by you. It is always the very same — every day.

This is creative meditation and it will work seeming miracles for you!

Learn this list of steps before you attempt to visit the miracle-producing theater of your mind:
1. Find a quiet spot in which you will not be disturbed.
2. You may sit in a comfortable chair or recline upon a bed or couch.
3. Relax completely.
4. Cleanse the mind.
5. Close the eyes.

6. Become mentally alert. Use your inner ear and your inner eye.
7. Write (mentally) your play carefully — once written, it cannot be changed with every rehearsal.
8. Visit your mental theater at least twice each day.
9. Act as if you are already your true self.
10. *Believe* it and it shall be so!

* * *

Creative meditation unfolded for me many, many years ago. I had started the smoking habit during my freshman year of college. Whatever I did in those days I did with all my might, and I was soon a pack-a-day smoker. After college I did want very badly to stop the habit, I would go for a few days — or at most a few weeks — without a single cigarette, then some seeming problem would break down my will power. This on and off routine lasted for twelve years! Then one day I realized that my little daughter — a first grader — was imitating me in her play. I certainly didn't want her to get the smoking habit too.

"Oh, if only I were — " and suddenly a picture came to mind. If only I were free of this habit, poised and very, very calm, I thought.

"You can be — for in truth you *are*," a small inner voice seemed to whisper.

Hearing those words, I slumped down in a big chair and wept — probably from a combination of frustration and hope. After the brief flood of tears, I began to really think about how I would look without a cigarette in my hand. While I was daydreaming, I saw a slimmer figure and a new hairdo. Why not? I thought. It's all good!

It was good and I enjoyed the thought immensely — so much so that I made a habit of sitting quietly in that same easy chair every day when I came home from work. In my mind I was calm and poised — no cigarette in sight! I was well-groomed and slim. I smelled fresh spring flowers. (Surely I could afford to buy some perfumes with all the money I would be saving on tobacco!)

I went to my mental theater each day and found a new calm enfolding me. I smoked less and less and in a few weeks none at all. I had in truth become the true me in my mental play. Never in all the years since have I ever desired a cigarette. I was, through creative meditation, completely healed!

* * *

By the time I went to my mental theater concerning employment, I was a much more experienced actress and director! Yet this was a challenge far greater than breaking a cigarette habit.

Due to a family situation I had given up my teaching position in the public schools at Thanksgiving, but by the following May it was necessary for me to support myself and my teen-age daughter. What would I do? One of the supervisors for the school system shook his head sadly and told me in strictest confidence that it would indeed be useless for me to apply for a position for the upcoming school year, since there was on file about one hundred applications for each vacancy. My heart sank. I looked around for other work — it was not the work I could do best, nor the pay which could provide any kind of living for my daughter and me.

How many years I had taught children to read! How much knowledge I had accumulated. What a waste if I could not ever help children learn ever again. With a new insight I made an appointment with the Superintendent of Personnel. We had a pleasant informal chat during which he assured me that *if* a vacancy occurred I would be the first to know about it. Encouragement but no contract!

I began writing a mental drama. This was going to be an extravanganza! There was a symphony playing in my inner ear — lights flashing then focusing in on center stage. I decided to have a large supporting cast of friends, relatives and well-wishers.

The drama began with me, the star, holding a contract to teach. I felt the thrill from head to toe and I always took a moment to say, "Thank You, Father!" I felt relief from anxiety and confident that my future would be financially secure. Next I heard my large cast wishing me well. Some called on the phone. I listened very intently as each voice told me that they had heard the news, that I would soon again be back in the classroom. Others met me on the street — in stores and after church. Next I visualized myself back in the classroom — working with children — presenting lessons — planning activities.

Whenever the thought came to mind that there were no vacancies, I immediately replaced it with the thought, "But there is a place for me! I know it! I feel it! I believe it!

Ten days later I received a contract and as of this writing I am still happily teaching.

Would I have been as successful had I imaged myself as a talented vocalist, ballet dancer or TV comic? No, hardly. For my true self would probably not have believed that drama.

I believe that whatever we have a deep desire to do or be we can do or be! We simply do not truly desire to be what we are not. An acorn is a future oak tree. A chicken egg is the beginning of a chicken. An unhappy, diseased person is in truth happy and whole!

"Maybe God wants me to suffer for a reason," some may lament. Why then did Jesus heal and make whole? The character of God is perfection and remember we are created in the image of God — of perfection!

Dare to be what you were created to be — happy, prosperous, healthy and fulfilled in every way!

*   *   *

Is it right to image for another? Well, certainly not for a specific thing — for even God does not do that in His great love and wisdom! However, it is always right to image good for others.

Some years ago a person very dear to me was desperately ill. For a few days I prayed sincerely for him not to die. I suddenly realized, however, that perhaps his soul had a different plan. So I changed my prayers and prayed for good only. I pictured him many times a day smiling, joyous, and free. I also silently spoke to him many times each day saying, "You are receiving your highest good."

He did not die. He surprised the doctors and made a speedy recovery. But had it been his time to pass on, he still would have been happy, joyous and free.

That is our only duty to others — to declare and pray for their highest good always.

* * *

Are you ready to go to the theater within and start changing your life? It need not be a great earth-shaking change — just a skit will do nicely for a beginning.

If you are a parent, you may like to share this technique of meditation with your children. Young children delight in it! You can help them gain in self-confidence — in their ability to get along with others — and to achieve in their school work.

And never fail to give thanks, dear reader, for our ability to think — to pray — to meditate — to change all things to good!

God Bless You!

About the author:

Serene West has been writing and lecturing on meditation for over thirteen years. She currently writes on the subject for *Unity Magazine, Aspire* and *Science Mind,* and produces a series of new age format greeting cards and cassette tapes on the uses of meditation for healing. Mrs. West holds a B. F. A. from the Richmond Professional Institute of the College of William and Mary (now Virginia Commonwealth University), and resides with her family in Chesapeake, Virginia.

The Unilaw Library Series

Unilaw Library is a line of inspirational, metaphysical and religious books which demonstrate the basic compatability of classic religious principles with ancient and modern metaphysical cosmology. The line will include fiction, children's books and practical, self-help applications. The purpose of Unilaw Library is to draw from all disciplines which contribute to the evolution of human thought, from the latest scientific discoveries to the use of intuitive process in creativity, and to contribute to the re-thinking of old dogmas and attitudes which will lead humanity to the truth about the nature of life and the universe.